The Ugly Christmas Sweater

Coloring Book For Adults

* Test page at end of book

Published By
Inspirational Wares
© 2016 Penelope Pewter

The back of each coloring page has a black backing to protect against bleeding when using markers or ink pens.

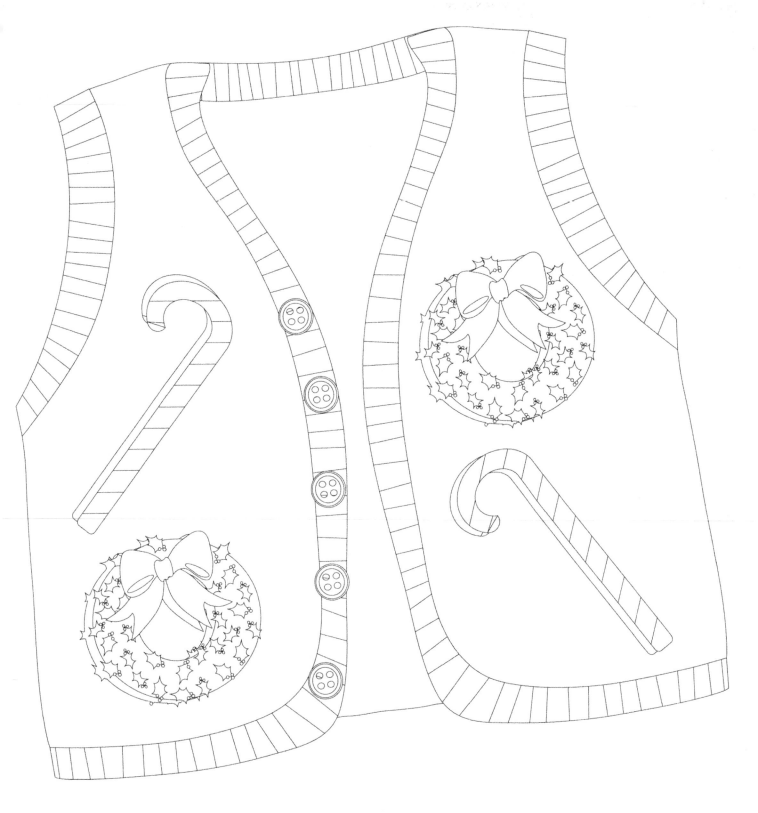

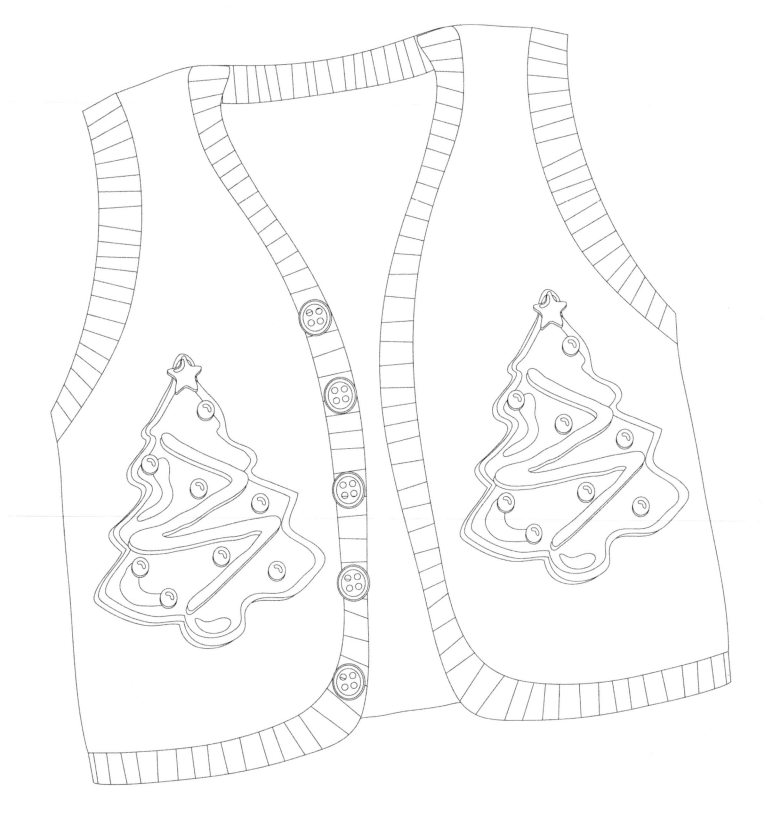

Test Page

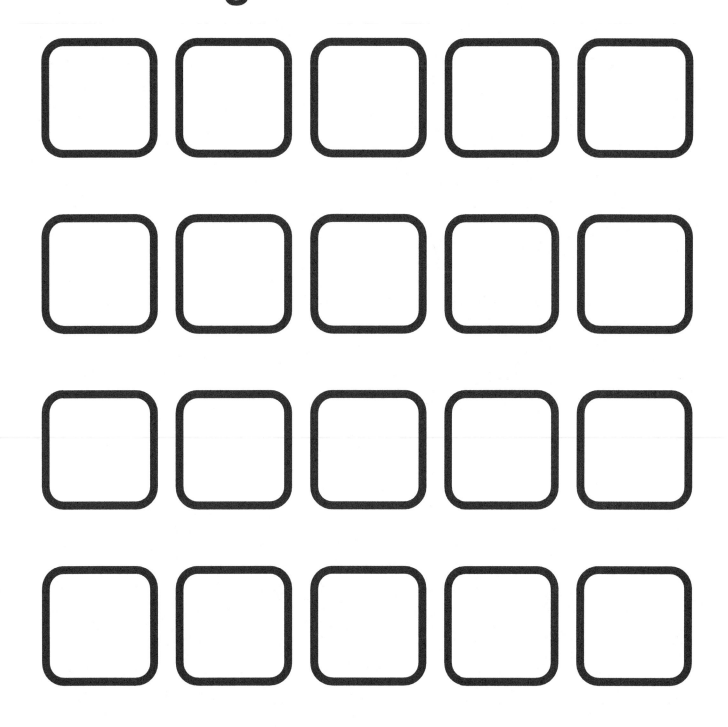

Other amazing adult coloring books available online at:
Amazon.com
CreateSpace.com
InspirationalWares.com

She Believed She Could
So She Did Adult Coloring Book

YOGA An Adult Coloring Book

The Matryoshka Nesting Doll
Coloring Book for Adults

The Ultimate Adult Coloring Book
for Men

Made in the USA
Coppell, TX
18 November 2019

11375548R00044